MW01610743

Atrocities Committed By ISIS in Syria & Iraq: ISIL/Islamic State/Daesh

Table of Content

Introduction

War is a state of incessant conflict when the legal codes and moral laws that govern interactions in civil society are turned on their heads and momentarily cease to exist.

Since the beginning of recorded history, some of the most atrocious crimes have been committed under the shadow of war and anarchy. In some instances, these war-time barbarous acts, such as the Nazi genocide of Jews, the Hiroshima/Nagasaki nuclear bombings and the 9/11 attack on the World Trade Center, have had the effect of completely altering the course of history.

The rise of the Islamic State of Iraq and Syria (ISIS) and the corresponding wars in the Middle East has been no exception to this rule. These Sunni jihadist militants have expressed their desire for political self-determination in extremely brutal ways that has left the world horrified. Over the past few months, the media has been flooded with images of decapitations, mass executions and other heinous activities by this group. These atrocities have subsequently attracted widespread condemnation - even from fellow hard line terrorists, such as al Qaeda, who have since disowned the new terrorist organization. The extent of the rapacious brutality of this group has forced World leaders to quickly authorize air strikes on the Islamic States' weapon stockpile and top leaders in a bid to stifle their rise.

Security experts say the Islamic State has since outdone its predecessors to become the most barbarous terrorist organization in recent history. According to these experts, the gruesome actions of Islamic State militants plays an intricate part in the group's propaganda and is sensationally calculated to bring recognition and clout to the comparatively new terrorist organization. The joint international military campaign against this religious militant organization has the potential to usher in a new level of co-operation and conflict resolution if the Assad regime, which has been battled by western-supported rebels, is able to collaborate with the same western governments. For the moment, it seems like an unlikely prospect - but one that will be welcomed by both sides.

It is clear that the ongoing war will completely alter the geographical and social outlook of the people of Iraq, Syria and the Levant. The Islamic State has sought to gain legitimacy and appeal among Muslims by declaring itself a caliphate. This has been a largely successful strategy and there is evidence of the outpouring of support for the Islamic State. But, on the other hand, this move has cemented the stereotypical association of the Islamic religion with radicalism. There is already lot of evidence of the militarization of civilians by both government and rebel forces in this war, which has been centered on territorial control. Meanwhile, many Arab nations, including Saudi Arabia, Egypt and the United Arab Emirates, have shown support for the joint military campaign against the Islamic State led by the United States.

While there is every inclination that World leaders will attempt to hold the Islamic State' figure-heads responsible for their atrocities, there are a lot of questions about the ability of the Iraqi judicial system to do this effectively and the effects of such trials may have in replanting the seeds of terrorism in the region. The future is uncertain, and all that is guaranteed is that the Middle East and the Islamic religion will never be the same.

In this book, we'll discuss the atrocities of the Islamic State (IS) to understand the group's cause. We'll also look at why this admittedly fundamentalist organization has chosen extreme brutality to convey their grievances and what lasting effects this war will have on the region.

The Atrocities of ISIS

The rise of the Islamic State has ushered in a new level of viciousness among terrorists, which has not been witnessed since the reign of al Qaeda's notorious founder Abu Musab al-Zarqawi between the late 20th and early 21st century. The numerous atrocities of ISIS include armed attacks on civilians, decapitations of deemed enemies and the imposition of stringent moral codes on people under their jurisdiction.

Unlike other terrorist groups, the atrocities of ISIS have not been limited to the government and western powers, but these Sunni jihadist militants have targeted Kurds, Christians and Shiite Muslims as well as some Sunni groups who are deemed to profess and practice that which is different from conventional Islamic teachings or who simply represent a threat to the spread of the new caliphate.

The origin of the violent rise of ISIS over the past few months is intricately connected with the internal strife in post-war Iraq. The cracks in the transitional government of Iraq under the United Iraqi Alliance (UIA) were apparent during the last few weeks of the reign of Ibrahim al-Eshaiker al-Jafari as the Prime Minister of the transitional government.

Al-Jafari, who was initially the vice president of the Transitional Government of Iraq, received the mandate to become Prime Minister of the country in 2005. But many Kurds and Sunnis protested the nomination of a Shia to lead the country. According to these dissenters, the transitional government had failed to end the protracted Iraqi war and therefore lost their right to request more time in charge of the affairs of the fragile country. Some commentators have speculated that the overblown discord, which reared its head in Iraq, had since been lurking in the shadows. The opposition to al-Jafari's nomination by Kurds and Sunni politicians and the general population is really the starting point of the ISIS-led sectarian conflict in the region.

Rather ominously, a few months before the elections that confirmed the UIA's claim to the leadership of Iraq, the government had put a new constitution into effect. The new constitution, which basically sets out the framework for a federalized system of government, was one of the ways the UIA had sought to end the deep sectarian conflict that pervades Iraqi society.

In the heat of the national debate over the leadership of the country, the al-Askari Mosque, one of the holiest Shia shrines in the country, was attacked by unknown militants, later identified to be al Qaeda. It is important to note that at this point, ISIS had not been disowned by al Qaeda, and many pundits have asserted that the tactic of attacking fellow Muslims resonates more with ISIS than it does with the current al Qaeda leadership.

The attack on the Samarra mosque sparked nationwide clashes between Sunni and Shite Iraqis. Reports indicate that hundreds of Sunni mosques were attacked by Shiite mobs. At the end of the 6 days long riot, which had forced the authorities to impose a daytime curfew, Iraqi officials say about 379 people had been killed and 458 injured. This was the

first known attack by the
group known as ISIS today.

This violence incident led to
a series of clashes in Iraq,
which culminated in the
famous bombing of the Shia,
populated Sadr City in
Baghdad in November 2006.
This attack has been
described as the most
devastating experience
Baghdad has endured since the
US invasion of Iraq in 2003.
The year 2006 marked the
beginning of the atrocities
committed by ISIS.

According to the United
Nations, over 34,000 people
were killed in the country
that year alone.
Interestingly, 2006 also saw
the deaths of al Zarqawi and
Saddam Hussein at the hands
of the United States.

Between 2006 and the
withdrawal of US forces from
Iraq in 2011, ISIS militants
under al Qaeda were

responsible for several
suicide attacks on Shia
populated areas and Christian
targets, which claimed
thousands of lives. Suicide
bombing as a guerilla tactic,
which had been adopted by al-
Zarqawi, subsequently spread
to other radical groups. Many
hard line Sunni militant
groups emerged in the country
around this period. These
attacks and other violent
actions by Sunni groups had
the effect of strengthening
the union of Shiite and Kurds
against the Sunni minority.

These militants continued to
carry out widespread attacks
against Shiite targets
throughout 2013. Reports
indicate that hundreds of
civilians lost their lives
during that tumultuous year.

Throughout this period, there
were many protests by Sunni
civilians against
marginalization by the
government. While some

historians have connected
this with the rise of ISIS
and the atrocious deeds of
this group, it is clear that
this is an oversimplification
of the circumstances
surrounding the rise of this
group, which is widely
regarded as the most
successful terrorist
organization of its time.

By mid-2013, many opinionists
had begun to describe the
situation in Iraq as full-
blown sectarian warfare. The
armed militants ventured
beyond simple suicide attacks
and mounted daring raids on
villages. Meanwhile, the
terrorists continued to
target Shiite civilians in
their raids. Officials say
over 7,000 people were killed
in the country that year.

This is how this period,
which has been described as
the bloodiest in the history
of the country, shaped itself
out. In the beginning of this

year, the Iraqi government ceded ground to the increasingly desperate Sunni militants in Anbar. Since ISIS militants captured Nineveh in June this year, there have been many reports of rape. Local sources say the terrorists have ordered all unmarried women to have sex with militants as a way of fulfilling their 'jihad' duty.

A decree released by the group only two days after taking over Nineveh reads "After liberation of the State of Nineveh, and the welcome shown by the people of the state to their brotherly mujahideen, and after the great conquest, and the defeat of the Safavid troops in the State of Nineveh, and its liberation, and Allah willing, it will become the headquarters for the mujahideen. Therefore we request that the people of this state offer their unmarried women so that they can fulfill their duty of jihad by sex to their brotherly mujahideen. Failure to comply with this mandate will result in enforcing the laws of Sharia upon them."

Similar decrees have been published in other places under the control of the terrorists in Iraq and Syria. Also, local sources say ISIS militants have imposed a special tax known as *jizya* on Christians and other non-Muslims in areas under their control. This special tax is seen as a scheme by the group to put more pressure on members of other religious groups, who are already forced to contend with many social restrictions, to convert to Islam.

It is interesting to note the contradiction in the words and deeds of the terrorists. While ISIS has ordered all women — non Muslims alike —

in areas under its control to
don a veil at all times,
reports indicate that people
who are found to be violating
this directive are often
caned or raped. It begs to
question if these laws are
really intended to promote
public decency and religious
chastity.

In addition to these
violations of the rights of
non-Muslims and Shiite
civilians, ISIS militants
have sought to impose a
minimum wage on all of these
civilians and to control
their access to basic
amenities such as electricity
and water. Local sources say
the homes and businesses of
many Christians and non-
Shiite Muslims have been
illegally confiscated by ISIS
since the insurrection
commenced. The ravaging
militants have also targeted
Churches and other historical
monuments for destruction.

Perhaps, the most heinous crimes of ISIS militants have been their extrajudicial executions of allegedly guilty individuals. Hundreds of Kurds, Shiite and Christians have been decapitated by the blood of thirsty terrorists. Videos released by the terrorists show them in a light hearted mood carrying out these barbarous atrocities. The most notable of these executions has been those of westerners – Steven Scotloff, James Foley and David Haines. Reports indicate that although the use of child soldiers have not been documented in this war, children have been recruited into the ranks of ISIS and have participated in the group's brutal decapitation of its prisoners.

ISIS militants have also conducted mass circumcisions of Christian males in areas under their control. In

August, an unknown number of men were forcefully circumcised without any anesthetic in Mosul. Meanwhile, security experts have revealed that ISIS is involved in human trafficking. The group has reportedly sold hundreds of women and girls in public auctions to traders, who are believed to transfer them to eager terrorist buyers in Afghanistan.

Apart from these atrocities, ISIS has also been charged with several economic crimes. Many local sources have revealed that ISIS militants openly loot the homes and offices of Christians and non-Sunni Muslims in areas under their control. The fact that civilians continue to flee their homes once they get wind of the arrival of the terrorists has supported their pillaging tendency. Also, reports indicate that ISIS has been controlling oil fields in its territory and selling petroleum in the black market to European buyers. This is thought to be one of the primary sources of funding for the terrorists.

The situation in Iraq and Syria is indeed a delicate one that threatens to topple over at the slightest inclination. With armed militant groups squaring off against one another, it is not unlikely that there will be a civil war in the region between ISIS and the authorities, as well as against other terrorist organizations it trampled on during its speedy rise to the center of the world's attention.

A report by the UN released in August accuses both the Syrian government and Islamic State rebels of committing crimes against humanity. According to the report, which is based in nearly 500 interviews and other informative materials, ISIS militants conduct frequent executions of alleged enemies or infidels. Officials say, that women also are often lashed by ISIS militants for allegedly failing to adhere to the strict codes they are provided. The atrocities of ISIS, as we have seen, border on dictatorial and barbaric tendencies.

Media Coverage of ISIS

The rise of the Islamic State
has received ample coverage
from the world's media not
only due to the news
worthiness of the objectives
of this ascending power, but
also because ISIS has relied
on barbarous actions to gain
attention and convey its
propaganda. The media has
indeed been very instrumental
in spreading the terror and
sectarian instigation wrought
by these radical Sunni
jihadists.

The Islamic State has
generally been portrayed in
the western media as an enemy
of democracy and social
justice. Many critics argue
that media outlets have
oversimplified the fact that
the Islamic State is - for
the most part - an Iraqi

institution which has set out
to settle a national dispute.
Instead, the group has been
painted as a vestige of
Middle Eastern terrorism that
seeks to topple the weak
government of post war Iraq.

Although there has been no
live coverage from inside the
country, many journalists
have reported from the
borders of neighboring
countries; where scores of
refugees fleeing fighting in
their homeland have
retreated. Due to the
unconventional sources of
information about ISIS, news
about the activities of this
group has in many instances
been inaccurate. Media
outlets have been accused of
trumpeting the propaganda of
ISIS in an attempt to report
on the gruesome Hollywood-
like documentaries released
by this group.

The widespread false reportage about ISIS has, without question, supported the group's rise to the center of international focus. Critics say that although rumors - such as the alleged takeover of Baghdad by the terrorists - are eventually deflated as the truth emerges, they nonetheless serve to sensitize the people about the war being waged by ISIS and military might of the rising power. Ultimately, this supports the purpose of the radical Islamists to spread terror and impose a new paradigm.

The media coverage of the war in Baghdad has been diverse: with both sides equally represented by their propaganda machines. While the authorities have controlled most of the

traditional media outlets,
the terrorists have relied on
new and unconventional forms
of broadcasting their
messages (i.e. social media).

In June, Iraqi officials
barred access to some of the
world's foremost news and
social media websites
including Twitter, YouTube
and Facebook. Although Iraqi
authorities claim the ban was
lifted after only about two
weeks, many witnesses have
complained of difficulties
accessing some websites,
several months after the ban
was supposedly lifted.

Sensationalism has been a
feature of wartime reporting
in Iraq. Sometimes reporters
ventured beyond this to
deliberately mislead the
people with false
information. The United
Nations High Commission for

Refugees (UNHCR) is one of
the institutions that
cautioned reporters in the
country against promoting
incentive stories that
compromises attempts to end
the raging war.

In the Arab world, the same
dividing lines characterized
the coverage of ISIS. Reports
indicate that several
journalists quit from popular
news stations in Iraq
(including ANB, Al-Hadath and
Al-Arabiya) during the onset
of the fighting in protest
against their employer's
skewed reporting policies
about the conflict.

The reaction of the Iraqi
government to being thrust in
the spotlight has been rather
interesting. While many pro-
government media outlets
carried the official
propaganda of the state, the

authorities have attempted to stifle the operations of opposing media houses. Also, the Iraqi government has sought to control the flow of information about the ongoing conflict. Reports indicate that several media houses – including the BBC – have been served with a notice by the government warning it against spreading false information. Iraqi officials have generally tightened their grip on the media and also attempted to curb access to some websites by the general public. But this has spurred claims from some opposition groups that the government is dictatorial.

In April, the Iraqi government passed the National Safety Law, which among other things empowers the state with the right to censor all publications before they are published or broadcasted. The law also stipulates that the authorities are permitted to use force to preserve public order, including confiscating copies of publications, preventing the broadcast or publication of an offending material and shutting down the premises of a publication, which is deemed to pose a threat to public security.

In June, the spokesman for the Iraqi military, Lieutenant General Qasim Ata, cautioned the press to ensure they report accurately on the events that transpired in the country. He accused the BBC Arabic of relying on unofficial sources for their information about the happenings in the country. Lt. Gen Ata is reported to have threatened to "take measures" to respond to any report that threatens the citizens of the country. Meanwhile, there are unconfirmed reports that the Iraqi authorities had been covertly monitoring anti-government media outlets in the country and throughout the entire region.

It was around this time that the National Communication and Media Commission of Iraq published a 9-point guideline for coverage of the crisis in the country. According to the commission, some local and international media outlets had been playing into the hands of the terrorists by broadcasting the rumors and half-truths generated by their propaganda machine. The commission therefore charged reporters with the following.

To hold themselves to the highest possible standard of professionalism and neutrality in covering security-related events, abide by the profession's behavioral norms so as to maintain the country's sovereignty and security, and refrain from broadcasting news material that may be interpreted against security forces, or broadcasting visual material that may harm them.

To focus on the security achievements of the armed forces, by repetition throughout the day, and highlighting them in special newscasts and coverage, praising the heroic acts performed by security personnel. And also to broadcast material showing the brutality of the enemy, and genuine news of the desperation and bankruptcy of the armed, terror groups.

To focus on the courageous, historical fatwa of the Supreme Guide Ali Sistany, giving it a patriotic character, and linking it to similar fatwas from Sunni men of learning, such as that of Sheikh Kabissy and other esteemed ulema.

It is absolutely forbidden, under any circumstances and even accidentally, to broadcast the messages of armed groups or their savage acts, to interview their members or to use material taken from international agencies with similar content. Do not seek a "scoop" at the expense of your country and its security.

It is absolutely forbidden to broadcast messages, information or breaking news that may lead to the targeting of security forces, the uncovering of their positions or the identification of their areas of deployment, thereby giving terrorists a "free service" while trying to attack them or instigating attacks on them.

It is absolutely forbidden to conduct live or recorded interviews, personally or via satellites, with individuals who are wanted by the law, or who head armed groups or adopt an inciting and escalating discourse, or who harm national security or disclose military or security-related classified information.

To absolutely refrain from broadcasting audio-visual material that may create an atmosphere of hostility between the elements of the Iraqi people, or lead to the targeting of any of those elements.

To hold on to the patriotic sense, and be careful when broadcasting material that may harm that sense, abiding by professional balance in cases where angry mobs, or program guests, may express insulting sentiments. It is necessary in such cases to indicate that such sentiments do not accord with the moral and patriotic order required for the war on terror.

To focus in news coverage on professionalism and patriotism, and to broadcast programs that spread enthusiasm and a fighting spirit against terror, in addition to patriotic anthems and the broadcasting of teeming crowds, and the heroic deeds of our security forces.

This 'draconian' directive has attracted widespread criticisms from many advocacy groups including Human Rights Watch. The activism body's deputy director for the Middle East and North Africa, Joe Stork, dismissed the guidelines as "a clear attempt to prevent critical coverage of important events and silence debate as the country goes through this intense security and political crisis." He also noted that the directive effectively prevents the press from completing the duty of reporting on the latest events and instead attempts to make the media the "public relations appendage" of the government.

Several journalists and media houses have revealed to investigators that the Iraqi government occasionally threatened them with revoking their operational license if they continued to present the news in a way that is contrary to the demands of the authorities.

Sometime in June, the Egyptian government barred some Iraqi stations operating in the country after receiving complaints from Baghdad. The head of the Egyptian broadcasting regulation body Free Zone revealed that "Al-Baghdadia and Al-Rafidain channels were taken off Nilesat for violating their contracts with the Free Zone authority regarding their content."

Reports indicate that the pro-Sunni media houses had made anti-government remarks and hailed the rise of the Sunni-dominated Islamic State in Iraq.

According to the general manager of Al Arabiya, whose station was threatened with closure by Iraqi authorities, "[Prime Minister] Maliki wants to punish Al-Arabiya as he did when he closed a large number of newspapers during the past few years only because those media outlets criticized his policies."

Meanwhile, Iran's Fars News Agency accused the Arabic press of waging "psychological warfare against the Iraqi people and government." The state owned publication charged several media houses (including Al Arabiya, Al Jazeera, BBC

Arabic and Sky News) of exaggerating the might of the terrorists as well as inciting division and promoting anti-American sentiments.

The unsurpassed ability of ISIS to recruit foreigners to join its ranks has been attributed to the groups' masterful use of the media – particularly social media. Since the beginning of the war in Iraq in 2003, terrorists have relied on social media to broadcast their ideals and make announcements. However, ISIS has taken the use of social media to a new level by using it as a recruitment tool.

According to the European Union anti-terrorism chief Gilles de Kerchove, ISIS is believed to have used social media to recruit a majority of the 3000+ Europeans estimated to be its ranks. Experts have described the terrorists' use of social media as "sophisticated and effective." The group is reported to use social media to spread news of its victories in the battle field, thereby increasing their credibility in jihadist circles and building fervor in fighters abroad for the 'cause.' Many experts agree the group has a team of social media experts who are in charge of its communication on these modern platforms. That some of the accounts linked to ISIS have up to 30,000 followers is a testament to the widespread influence of this group. A community of online jihadists has sprung up over the past few years. Many openly discuss internal issues with their colleagues, such as the availability of Internet or beautiful women in particular place. So-called fighters have also used social media to spread the group's propaganda by recounting the benefits they have gained since joining the group.

In response to the successful use and manipulation of the media, there have been many calls for a media blackout of all things related to ISIS. According to these pundits, the widespread public debate and republication of their messages and horrific actions serves into the interest of the terrorists as it increases their profile.

ISIS use of the media has been very powerful. The blacklisted organization has been able to keep its ranks active and spread its message using the media. Many pundits have noted that the world's media have aided rather than tackled this anti-democratic scourge. ISIS' adept use of social media may easily be the most advanced display of manipulation the world has witnessed from Islamic extremists.

The World's Response to ISIS

The reaction to the rise of
the Islamic Caliphate has
differed according to the
geographical, religious and
political affiliations of the
individuals and nations in
question.

In the west, the general
reaction to ISIS has been one
of bewilderment and horror.
The repeated broadcast of
footages showing ISIS
beheading western nationals
served to carve a savage
image for this group. Many
have described ISIS as a
modern militant group that
has set out to establish a
society based on draconian
medieval ideology.

Several American Muslims have
held public conferences to
delineate themselves from
ISIS and condemn the gruesome
actions of the group.
According to these Muslims,
the actions of ISIS

contravene the teachings of
the Qu'ran. The religious
leader of the Islamic House
of Wisdom Dearborn Heights
Michigan Imam Elahi has
described ISIS as a "bunch of
gangsters." Imam Elahi also
explained that the actions of
the group have no backing in
the Islamic holy book.

Overall, the headline-
grabbing rise of ISIS
rehashed long buried anti-
Muslim sentiments from the
9/11 era. But many Muslims in
the west have striven to
delineate themselves and
their religion from this
scourge. Alia Almulla, an
Iraqi citizen in America,
explains that terrorism is
not part of the doctrines of
the Qu'ran. "People need to
become more educated about
Islam and actually read the
Qu'ran. Until you actually
read the Qu'ran, don't
judge," he says.

Christians in the country have been appalled by this growing power, which is overtly opposed to their faith. Despite the ongoing offensive, many people have blamed President Obama for failing to do more to stop ISIS. According to these critics, the failure of Washington to act quickly during the crucial first few days and weeks that this terrorist group began their insurrection ensured they were able to overwhelm the local security and impose their dominance on about a third of Syria and a quarter of Iraq.

In August, President Obama made a live speech to the American people in whom he explained the necessity of military intervention in Iraq and Syria against ISIS. According to the president, U.S. interests as well as religious and ethnic minorities were being severely threatened by the rise of ISIS. Reports indicate that the group has targeted many corporate facilities and also killed hundreds of Yazidi Christians, Kurds and other minorities in the country.

While officials have explained that the reason for the slow reaction to the rise of ISIS is because the country's military is overstretched. This is reportedly also one of the reasons why the US has only offered to support the local forces with air strikes and the president insists ground forces will not be deployed to the country where they left after many years of fighting only a few years ago. On the other hand, critics of the US say President Obama chose not to respond quickly to ISIS because the group's destructive actions were in line with the US objectives.

According to this school of
thought, the US government
had become disillusioned with
Iraq under the leadership of
former Prime Minister Nouri
al-Maliki and therefore
covertly rejoiced at the rise
of the de-stability that led
to his abdication. Critics
also say that the President
Obama and the west have not
'come down hard' on ISIS
because the group has
targeted countries who are
opposed to the US and western
influence. These opinionists
say the state of things will
change sharply when ISIS
begins to attack allies of
the west, such as Israel.

Similarly in Britain and
across Europe, several Muslim
individuals and organizations
have come out to strongly
censure ISIS and distance
themselves from the group.
The reaction to this group in
other parts of the world –
such as Britain, Europe and

Saudi Arabia – has been notably complicated.

While there have been an outpouring of anti-ISIS sentiments, which is exemplified by a letter from several prominent British Muslims leaders to David Cameron sometime in mid-September urging him to reassess the use of the word 'Islamic' to describe the brutal jihadists. According to these opinion leaders, the continued reference to the terrorists as the Islamic State plays into their intent to build legitimacy among Muslims across the world by posing as a sort of promise land. Reports indicate that this strategy of the terrorists has chalked considerable success as many British, European and Saudi Muslims thronged to fill their ranks during the first few months of the insurrection. Investigators say some hard-line Muslims across the world are believed to be sustaining ISIS by funneling thousands of dollars to the group monthly. Several hundred British Muslims are believed to have departed to join the ranks of jihadists in Syria and Iraq over the past few years. Experts say this number has spiraled dramatically since the rise of ISIS a few months ago.

In an attempt to explain the rise of Islamic radicalism in the country that has seen several individuals depart for uncertainty in the Middle East, many experts have speculated that these sentiments must have been pre-existing in the British society but perhaps concealed. Although there have been many foiled terrorist schemes in the country, there hasn't really been an attack the scale of 9/11.

On the flip side, the Home Office has warned that the extremely brutal actions of the Islamic State are fuelling Islam phobia in the country. An unidentified officer told the BBC Radio 4 during an interview in September that the repercussion of the actions of ISIS in British society is real and worrying. "I have been working with people from the far-right for about 27 years now, I can see increases in some of these groups and membership in some of these groups based on things that are happening nationally here and internationally," he told the interviewer.

A report by the Daily Mail reveals that many Briton jihadists in Syria are desperate to return to their home country after becoming disillusioned with the life of crime. The report noted that about 500 Britain nationals have travelled to Syria to join the war between President Bashar Assad and the rebels in the past three years. Some of the fighters in the ranks of the rebels are reported to have contacted British authorities and expressed their eagerness to return home. The terrorists claim they sought to join the Syrian people fight against an authoritarian regime, but have ended up becoming involved in a sort of "gang warfare." Monash's University's Professor Greg Barton, who studied the trend of young British Muslim departing from their country to be jihadists, concluded that these "young men" who he described as having "fairly juvenile mentality" are "driven by peer pressure and desire for affirmation."

Officials say more than 200 British nationals have attempted to return home from their jihadist mission in Syria and have been put in the clutches of the authorities. Experts estimate that up to a thousand British nationals could be in the ranks of ISIS. According to these experts, several public announcements of ISIS – notably the cold blooded decapitation of a Briton and two Americans – has been done by people with unmistakable British accents.

Another evidence of the strong influence of British nationals in the Islamic State came in a tape announcement by one of the group's leaders Abu Mohammad al-Adnani, during which he described the US Secretary of State – who had been rallying support against the group throughout the world – as an 'uncircumcised old geezer.' The significance of this statement is in the use of the word 'geezer' which is a common British slang betrayed the fact that the speaker was British or his speech was written by a British national. Meanwhile, many experts have also underlined that fact that the masked executioner in the gruesome videos released by the terrorists spoke with a British accent before he committed his cold bloody decapitation of the prisoners.

Although the FBI and British intelligence officials confess that they have been able to identify the masked man, who has since been renamed 'Jihadi John', the authorities have hesitated from disclosing the identity of the suspect or contacting his relatives – at least just yet. Officials say more information is being gathered on the suspect and his links to his relatives and other acquaintances. Meanwhile, some pundit say the authorities may have covertly interrogated the relatives of the suspect and may be simply shunning from disclosing this fact to the public to protect the identity of the individuals concerned – who may not have any connection with terrorism.

Fears of western jihadists on the frontline in Iraq and Syria influencing their friends and relatives back home to commit terrorist acts has been highlighted by various western governments. In September, the Australian Police conducted what has been described as its largest anti-terror raid on Muslim populated neighborhoods in Sydney and Brisbane. According to the officials, the raid was precipitated by intelligence gathering that Australians in the ranks of ISIS are ordering their comrades back home to stage a "demonstration killing."

US officials have since disclosed that intelligence reports indicate ISIS had intended to carry out a large scale attack in a western nation in September 2014 to mark the 13th anniversary of the attack on the World Trade Center in New York on Sept. 11. 2000. Many security experts have seconded this assertion that the terrorist are more likely to conduct an attack on a western target than on an Arab one in order to raise their profile. The danger of the probability of a terrorist attack in Europe has been increased by the more complex reaction of the society to the rise of the so-called modern Caliphate.

The British Prime Minister David Cameron has revealed that ISIS has attempted about 6 unsuccessful attacks against European nations. "The point I would make even today to the British people is: be in no doubt about the threat that so-called Islamic State poses to us. We have already seen something like six planned attacks in the countries of the European Union from [IS]. Including of course that appalling attack in the Brussels Jewish museum, where innocent people were killed. That flows directly from this organization," he said.

The European Union security chief Gilles de Kerchove has also echoed these concerns. According to him, it is "very likely that ISIS … maybe is preparing, training, directing some of the foreign fighters to mount attacks in Europe."

In May 2014, shortly before the rise of ISIS in the Middle East, a 29-years old French national Mehdi Nemmouche held up the Jewish Museum in Brussels at gun point. Reports indicate that he shot at least four people:

three died and one survived. Investigators have since revealed that the suspect spent some time in Syria and is recorded to have connections with ISIS. This is considered the most successful attack by this Sunni jihadist group, in Europe to date.

Since then many pundits have theorized on the level of radicalization in France's large immigrant Islamic community. A poll released by ICM Research in August, which studied opinions from people in Germany, France and the UK, concluded that the French showed the most support for ISIS. Many pundits have since compared this to other polling result, which seems to prove that the French show more support for ISIS than Palestinians in Gaza. This is not really surprising if one considers the fact that the people of Gaza are deeply embroiled in a war for their homeland, while the migrant Muslim communities in France are largely escaping their homeland which they have become disillusioned with and are therefore more likely to support an Islamic State.

In September, a top ISIS operative Abu Muhammad al-Adnani urged followers of the group in Europe to attack western nationals. Mr. Kerchove has explained that these attacks are likely to be committed by returning jihadists like Nemmouche, in a pre-planned raid. Experts have since noted that about 3,000 western nationals – notably Europeans – are likely to be in the ranks of the terrorists. EU security officials have held several meetings over the past few months to iron out a strategy to counter this threat. One top European security official has revealed to the media that European security officials are "aware" and "frightened" by ISIS.

It is interesting to note that ISIS has gotten more support in Europe than the group has in some parts of the Middle East. Although critics have accused some Arab nations – such as Kuwait, Saudi Arabia and Qatar of covertly sponsoring the terrorists, the entire Arab world has reacted with bewilderment at the actions of ISIS. The fact remains that ISIS is perhaps the only group/organization in the Middle East today that is ready to sustain the sectarian warfare it instigated.

The rise of ISIS is threatening to rehash long buried lines of conflict in the Middle East and ultimately throw the entire region into instability. Many experts have noted that while Sunni dominated nations have

been accused of showing
support to the militants;
many Shia dominated nations
(such as Iran) have been in
the forefront of the
international effort to put
an end to the rise of ISIS.
Several Arab nations –
including some of those
accused of covertly
sponsoring the terrorists
like Saudi Arabia, Kuwait and
Qatar – have shown support
for the US-led initiative to
attack the group.

In Asia, the authorities have
been quick to stifle any
growing support for ISIS. In
August, the government of
Indonesia banned all citizens
from actively showing support
for ISIS. Indonesia is the
nation with the highest
population of Muslims in the
world; therefore this move
was seen as a direct blow to
the religious rooted
legitimacy claims of ISIS. At
least 56 Indonesian nationals
are believed to be in the

ranks of the terrorists. But officials claim all 56 men have since died in battle. The Security Affairs Minister Djoko Suyanto warned the public against the growing support for the jihadists.

It is interesting to note that ISIS has not taken root among the Islamic community in Indonesia, who are reportedly 99% Sunni. Many pundits say this may be due to the fact that Indonesian Muslims are considered moderate in comparison to their Middle Eastern companions. Meanwhile, the actions of the Indonesian government are thought to have been a part of a strategic plan to preserve the unity of the culturally and religiously diverse nation.

Reports indicate that the terrorists are attracting a throng of fighters from the

Asia-Pacific region. Many
ISIS-inspired militant groups
have sprung up in Indonesia
and Malaysia over the past
few months. In May, a rebel
group made up of a coalition
of fighters from Uzbekistan,
Russia, and Tajikistan and
across the entire Caucasus
swore allegiance to ISIS. The
group, known as Sabari's
Jamaat, reportedly swore
allegiance to ISIS to counter
the power of al Qaeda.
Although one Chinese national
is alleged to be in the ranks
of the terrorists, ISIS have
not succeeded in taking root
in mainland Asia.

The Future of Iraq and Syria

On Sept. 10, President Obama
announced the US counter
terrorism plans for ISIS. He
noted, "ISIL poses a threat
to the people of Iraq and
Syria, and the broader Middle
East - including American
citizen, personnel and
facilities." He went on to
note "If left unchecked,
these terrorists could pose a
growing threat beyond that
region - including to the
United States."
He went on to warn that
intelligence reports indicate
that "trained and battle-
hardened" European and
American fighters in the
ranks of ISIS could return
back to their countries and
commit terrorist acts.
Many things remain uncertain
in relation to the ongoing
battles in Iraq and Syria,
but one thing many pundits
seem to agree with is that it
will take more than air raids
to destroy ISIS. Despite the

best efforts of President
Obama to erase this
possibility, it seems it will
after all be the way out of
the ongoing crisis.
Nonetheless, the US President
has noted that the air
strikes "have protected
American personnel and
facilities, killed ISIL
fighters, destroyed weapons,
and given space for Iraqi and
Kurdish forces to reclaim key
territory. These strikes have
helped save the lives of
thousands of innocent men,
women and children," he said.

In September, the Speaker of
the House of Representatives
John Boehner confessed to ABC
during an interview that
troops on the ground is
inevitable at some point.
These same sentiments have
been expressed by many other
veteran politicians in the
country. Experts say besides
the overstretching of US
forces – which is only a ruse
to cover up the real issues

that public opinion is the main factor hindering the country's leadership from plunging into Iraq with ground forces. The role of the US in Iraq has been strongly criticized. Many groups have accused the country's leadership of escalating the severity of the threat and feigning the immediacy of the danger in order to excuse the invasion of Iraq in 2003. Public opinion polling groups have come out to state that their findings suggest a majority of the American people were not satisfied with the country's first involvement in Iraq and have pessimistic feelings about its latest incursion into that country. According to a poll quoted by Time.com, about 60% of all Americans are thought to have negative feelings about the first Iraqi war. This is a significant point because some commentators have noted that one of the primary reasons why President Obama has shunned from deploying ground forces to Iraq to fight ISIS is due to the negative public opinion about the consequences of this move as evidenced by the US Army's recently ended occupation of Iraq. A report by Military Times has also revealed that 70% of a group of 2,200 active duty troops also expressed negative opinion about another incursion into Iraq. Meanwhile, from all indications Congress will not table this topic until next year. Speaker John Boehner has told the press "Doing this [the contentious debate] with a whole group of members who are on their way out the door, I don't think that is the right way to handle this." Instead he noted that "I would suggest early next year, assuming that we continue in this effort, there may be that discussion and there may be that request from the president." It is highly likely that the US Congress will approve the deployment of troops to Iraq after all if one considers the following argument: From the current state of things, ISIS is bound to remain as strong or even grow in strength and territory between now and when Congress debates the topic next year. Meanwhile, the war against the group would continue. But, as many security experts have noted, the airstrikes are only going to incense the terrorists into committing more atrocious deeds, this would in turn raise negative public sentiments against the group and change the current perception that plunging into Iraq is wasteful and unnecessary.

This is the most likely outcome of the current stalemate as Gideon Rose in 'Endgame in Iraq' aptly writes "Assad might seem like he is in control, but his

troops rarely tangle with
ISIS, preferring instead to
take on the more moderate
factions. In fact, his regime
has only been able to go on
the offensive in western
Syria with the help of
Hezbollah, Iraqi Shia
militias, and Iran's Quds
force. When their support
disappears, so, too will
Assad's luck. For example,
when Iraqi Shia militiamen
were recently recalled from
the Lebanese-Syrian frontier
to fight ISIS in Iraq, Syrian
opposition forces quickly
reappeared, retook part of
the area and continued to
stage hit-and-run attacks. In
other words, Assad and the
rebels are at a stalemate
and, unless the West and its
Arab allies try something
new, the conflict will
persist."

The US-led coalition which
has been attacking ISIS in
Iraq and Syria includes the
following countries: Saudi

Arabia, United Arab Emirates, Bahrain, Qatar, Jordan, Belgium, Britain, Canada, Czech Republic, Australia, Denmark, France, Germany, Italy, Netherlands, Albania, Estonia, Hungary and Turkey. Meanwhile, the Russian government has offered to support Iraqi forces tackle the growing strength of the jihadists. Reports indicate that over 200 strikes have been made in Iraq and nearly 50 in Syria since the bombardments commenced in August. In mid September, the raid for the first time came close to the city of Baghdad after US forces attacked a terrorist target near the capital city of the country. The presence of stability in Baghdad is widely seen as a sort of 'litmus test' to determine the stability of the country. Recently, the terrorists have been making incursions towards that city. But officials remain optimistic that they can be kept away and the stability of Baghdad can be preserved.

The US-led attacks on ISIS in Syria have attracted some criticisms from the antagonistic Assad regime. Many rebels in the country have accused the US government of complicity aiding the Assad government's attempts to overpower them by suppressing the Islamic State. This is interesting to note because ISIS have waged war on virtually all the rebels groups fighting against Assad besides the al Nusra Front. Many experts say it is highly unlikely that Assad would respond aggressively to the attacks on his country. But a question looms about what effects this foreign military interference will have on Syria in the long term, i.e. if ISIS is suppressed what next, would the US resume its support for the rebels against Assad, and what form of support would this be?

US officials have revealed that the country's key strategy in Syria includes collaborating with and training moderate rebels to battle ISIS on the ground and subsequently the Assad regime. Recently the US Defense Secretary Chuck Hagel has told the press that "This will not be an easy or brief effort," he said, "We are at the beginning, not the end." Reports indicate that Congress has approved $500 to be used to support the efforts to train Syrian rebels. But experts say it will not be until about a year that the first groups of trainees are combat ready. This has raised many questions about the US government's commitment to the war. Many critics have also criticized the US government for becoming over involved in the war.

According to these pundits, it is a dubious undertaking to attempt to differentiate and support 'moderate' rebels in Syria. Many have urged the US government to provide its yardstick for differentiating between moderate rebels and their more extreme colleagues.

While many pundits regard it as a certainty that Iraq and Syria will be reclaimed from ISIS, some commentators have pushed the world to imagine the reverse of this eventuality, i.e. what happens if the US-led military offensive is unable to topple the jihad leadership and restore the territory under their control to democracy?

Interestingly, this outcome may not be as bad as it may look on the surface. For years, the ethnically and religiously diverse people of this region have been suffered to live under the tyranny of dictatorships. It is inevitable that the people would seek to correct the perceived ills wrought against them. The problem however is to what extend the attempts to resolve their grievances affect others. Some pundits say if the ISIS is able to withstand the military offensive against it, there is a chance that the world will be forced to contend with a new power in the Middle East. But the birth of this new power would simultaneously spell the beginning of a long period of warring in the region. Often attempts to describe the war in Iraq and Syria oversimplify the facts. It is a fact that the US-led coalition and the Iraqi Army are only a few of the adversaries lined up against the Islamic State. Since the war began a few months ago, several reports indicate that the Iranian Army has been involved in clashes with ISIS forces. Nonetheless, the Iranian government officially denies having military presence in the war-torn Iraq.

The Iranian government stands most to gain from the ongoing war. First, its intervention in Iraq has helped counter the prevailing perspective of the country as an aggressor. Due to Iran's proximity and interest in the war in Iraq, many pundits have noted that Iran is likely to be a key player in any foreign military intervention in Iraq. Now, the US government is being forced to reconcile with Iran and bring her back into the fray of international relations in order to effectually tackle ISIS. Insider reports indicate that officials from Iran and G-6 nations have been eagerly working to draw up an agreement that would safeguard and satisfy the interests of both sides. Currently, this seems highly unlikely, but it is almost guaranteed to be the case. Another reason why western powers are being forced to come to terms with Iran is to stop the spread of ISIS to their allies in the region. It is a fact that Iran has one of the most powerful militaries in the Middle East; therefore any major operation that is backed by it has greater chances of success. This eventuality has some real probability if we consider the fact that the air raids against the terrorists cost about $1 billion. Experts say the bill for the strikes could soar to as high as $2 to $4 billion in a year. The addition of ground forces is expected to take the cost of the war to about $13 to $22 billion. Many pundits have noted that the world powers will be looking to share the cost of this important war. Also, US officials have warned that the country's spending on war is overstretched. Therefore, the probability of Iran being dragged into the war seems quite high. If this happens, it is almost certain that ISIS will be destroyed. There is also a high chance that the Israeli Army will also participate in the war. But some pundits have warned that this could cause some partners of the coalition to withdraw.

Another potentially dangerous conflict is being formed between Kurdish fighters and the Iraqi Army. Both sides have collaborated to fight ISIS thus far and recorded many success. But experts say both sides have completely different objectives for becoming engaged in the war and these points of contention will begin to emerge once the threat of ISIS is contained. The Kurdish people, who are oppressed across the Middle East, have expressed their aspirations of forming an independent state. The fact remains that if these aspirations are not compactable with the democratic order, the Kurdish Army will be forced to pick up their arms to defend their rights and in so doing further the vicious cycle of terrorism in the region.

Conclusion

Like the ancient Egyptian deity whose name this group's acronym resonates with, ISIS represents the beauty and danger of devotion and nationalism. It remains to be seen if the revolution of the modern ISIS will be successful as it was later to be for the Ancient matriarch whose son reclaimed the stolen throne of his father. Indeed, many opinionists have warned that the war could linger on for many years if ISIS continues to receive buoyant support from its diverse sources.

In the words of Gideon Rose, the author of 'Endgame in Iraq', "The fight with ISIS is a regional conflict that requires a regional solution. It took a Central America-wide peace effort to end El Salvador's civil war and a similar collective approach to end Cambodia's genocidal war. Ultimately, the same is needed in Iraq (and Syria), but "friends" who could shepherd a peace process are in a short supply. Iran and some Arab state have waged a proxy war in Syria. To gain at least tacit consent for U.S. reengagement in Iraq, it will be necessary to appeal to their shared interests (along with Russia and Turkey) in denying ISIS a state. More optimistically, the ISIS crisis might provide a diplomatic opening to limit the flow of arms and funds across Syrian and Iraqi borders."

CPSIA information can be obtained at www.ICGtesting.com
Printed in the USA
LVOW05s0250051114

411991LV00031B/1793/P